DARE
TO
LOVE

8 REASONS TO LOVE YOU DARE

STEPHEN KENDRICK
ALEX KENDRICK
MICHAEL CATT

Presented To:

_____

_____

From:

_____

_____

LIFEWAY PRESS®
NASHVILLE, TENNESSEE

Published by LifeWay Press® © 2009 Sherwood Baptist Church

No part of this book may be reproduced or transmitted in any form or by any
means, electronic or mechanical, including photocopying and recording, or by
any information storage or retrieval system, except as my be expressly permitted
in writing by the publisher. Requests for permission should be addressed in
writing to LifeWay Press; One LifeWay Plaza; Nashville, TN 37234-0175.

ISBN 978-1-4158-6655-9 • Item 005222545

Dewey Decimal Classification: 220.07
Subject Heading: BIBLE–STUDY / LOVE / MARRIAGE

FIREPROOF © 2008 Sony Pictures Home Entertainment
© 2009 Sherwood Baptist Church of Albany GA, Inc. All Rights Reserved
© 2009 Layout and Design, Provident Films LLC. All Rights Reserved

Scripture quotations marked HCSB® are taken from the Holman
Christian Standard Bible®, copyright © 1999, 2000, 2002, 2003
by Holman Bible Publishers. Used by permission.

Scripture marked NASB are taken from the New American Standard Bible®,
Copyright © 1960, 1962, 1963, 1968, 1971, 1972, 1973, 1975, 1977, 1995 by
The Lockman Foundation. Used by permission. (www.lockman.org)

To order additional copies of this resource: WRITE LifeWay Church Resources
Customer Service, One LifeWay Plaza; Nashville, TN 37234-0113; FAX order to
(615) 251-5933; PHONE 1-800-458-2772; E-MAIL to orderentry@lifeway.com; ORDER
ONLINE at www.lifeway.com; or visit the LifeWay Christian Store serving you.

Printed in the United States of America
Leadership and Adult Publishing; LifeWay Church Resources;
One LifeWay Plaza; Nashville, TN 37234-0175

Contents

Introduction

The Love Dare cannot be taken lightly.

Marriage is challenging and often difficult, but can be incredibly fulfilling. To love someone for a lifetime requires a resolute mind and a steadfast determination. It is a commitment. Marital love is not meant to be sampled or briefly tested.

These eight reasons to take *The Love Dare* should remind you that love is worth fighting for. This booklet contains a sample of the powerful truths from *The Love Dare* journal and *The Love Dare Bible Study*. Living out these truths could change your life and your marriage.

If you search God's Word at the same time, it will change you for eternity.

Dare to love.
Take The Love Dare.

The Scriptures tell us that God created marriage as a good thing—a beautiful and priceless gift. God uses marriage to help us eliminate our loneliness, multiply our effectiveness, establish families, raise children, enjoy life, and bless us with relational intimacy.

Marriage also shows us our need to grow and deal with our own issues and self-centeredness through the help of a lifelong partner. If we are teachable, we will learn to do the one thing that is most important in marriage—to love.

This powerful union called marriage provides you the path to learn how to love another imperfect person unconditionally.

Marriage is wonderful, difficult, life-changing.

This book is about love and introduces you to how you can learn to love another person more completely.

The wisdom in this small book may be enough to show you that, with God's help:

You *can* lead your heart.

You *can* control the power of influence.

You *can* honor and cherish your spouse.

You *can* live with understanding.

You *can* give unconditional love.

You *can* walk in forgiveness.

You *can* build your marriage on prayer and God's Word.

You *can* establish a covenant marriage.

But not on your own …

You will discover why only God's love can equip you to meet the challenge and truly and selflessly love your spouse.

LOVE: THE SUPERIOR WAY

If I speak the languages of men and of angels,
but do not have love,
I am a sounding gong
or a clanging cymbal.

If I have [the gift of] prophecy, and understand all mysteries
and all knowledge,
and if I have all faith,
so that I can move mountains,
but do not have love,
I am nothing.

And if I donate all my goods
to feed the poor, and if I give my body
to be burned,
but do not have love,
I gain nothing.

1 CORINTHIANS 13:1-3, HCSB

*You Can Lead
Your Heart*

REASON 1

This small book is about love,
what it is and what it is not
(1 Corinthians 13).

It is about daring to love and
learning to live a life filled with
loving relationships.

Your journey begins with the person
who is closest to you:
your spouse.

Humorous episodes . . . dramatic scenes . . . thrilling mysteries still unfolding—we're all in different "acts" and "scenes" in our marriages.

No matter where you are with your spouse, you are on a journey of exploring and demonstrating genuine love, even when your desire is dry and your motives are low.

Moment by moment our culture bombards us with different messages about love. "Follow your heart" is the default advice of many books, movies, songs, plays, and television. Sound familiar? Yes, but it can be wrong nonetheless.

Following our hearts would be good if our hearts were always loving, in tune with God, and directed toward the right thing. However, since humans are self-centered, proud, and often deceived, following our hearts may not always lead us to do the right thing.

Every area of your life is impacted by the direction of your heart. Your heart follows your investments. Your investments are those things into which you pour your time, money, and energy.

Your investments draw your heart because they reflect your priorities. "*For where your treasure is, there your heart will be also*" (Matthew 6:21, HCSB).

Following your heart can mean chasing after whatever feels right at the moment. Emotions and feelings can be deceptive, leading you down the wrong path.

Marriages can be damaged or broken when one or both spouses insist it is their right to do whatever it takes to make them happy. *"If you have bitter envy and selfish ambition in your heart, don't brag and lie in defiance of the truth. Such wisdom does not come down from above, but is earthly, sensual, demonic"* (James 3:14-15, HCSB).

But you can lead your heart. You can learn to guide your heart by investing daily in your spouse, and your spouse can become your treasure. If you are not in love with your spouse today, it may be because you stopped investing in your spouse yesterday.

Leading your heart means to:

- Take full responsibility for your heart's condition and direction.

- Realize that you have control over where your heart is.

- Ask God for the power to guard or protect your heart by taking it off the wrong things and setting it on the right things.

A wise man said, "*Listen, my son, and be wise, and direct your heart in the way*" (Proverbs 23:19, NASB).

Love is a decision, not just a feeling. It is selfless, sacrificial, and transformational. And when love is truly demonstrated as intended, your relationship can change for the better.

Don't wait ... until doing the right thing feels right, until you feel in love with your spouse to set your heart and invest in your relationship.

Instead, start pouring yourself into your marriage now.

Start praying that God will:
- Grow you emotionally.
- Make you more intentional.
- Give you the power to change old habits.
- Break you free from old, unhealthy ways.

Ask the Master of our lives for help and courage to redirect the coordinates of your heart toward Him and toward your spouse. There you will find the most valuable treasures.

A Love Dare

Based on Dare 1 in The Love Dare Journal

ALTHOUGH LOVE IS COMMUNICATED IN
A NUMBER OF WAYS, OUR WORDS OFTEN
REFLECT THE CONDITION OF OUR
HEART. FOR THE NEXT DAY, RESOLVE TO
DEMONSTRATE PATIENCE AND TO SAY
NOTHING NEGATIVE TO YOUR SPOUSE
AT ALL. IF THE TEMPTATION ARISES,
CHOOSE NOT TO SAY ANYTHING. IT'S
BETTER TO HOLD YOUR TONGUE THAN
TO SAY SOMETHING YOU'LL REGRET.

LOVE NOTE: *Your heart follows your investment. Write
your spouse letters, long or short. Buy your spouse gifts. Spend
time together as a couple. Your heart will follow.*

You Can Control the
Power of Influence

REASON 2

If you are not leading your heart,
then someone or something
else is. The people you listen to and
the influences you allow
into your life affect your
destiny as a couple.

You can dare to live in kindness and patience with your spouse—one of the greatest and most worthy challenges of your life.

Love requires thoughtfulness on both sides—thoughtfulness that builds bridges through the constructive combination of patience, kindness, and selflessness. Love teaches us how to meet in the middle and how to respect and appreciate how our spouse uniquely thinks.

You have a God who is all-powerful, who will honor your commitment to your marriage, and who exhorts: "*Therefore, submit to God. But resist the Devil, and he will flee from you*" (James 4:7, HCSB).

Would you be surprised to discover that the success of your marriage is directly related to the influences around you?

Who or what influences you?

Who or what is whispering in your ear?

Are your closest friends champions for or enemies of your marriage?

Anyone who undermines your marriage does not deserve to be called a friend. Anyone who discourages your goal of fireproofing your marriage is not giving you good advice. Anyone who urges you to yield to temptation as something you deserve or cannot resist is a friend who is not really on your side.

How do you filter your friends? Learn to choose your friends carefully. They always influence you, one way or another.

Keep these words in mind:

"No temptation has overtaken you except what is common to humanity. God is faithful and He will not allow you to be tempted beyond what you are able, but with the temptation He will also provide a way of escape."

1 Corinthians 10:13, HCSB

A wise spouse recognizes influences that could harm his or her marriage. Some are much easier to spot than others.

Recognizing the subtle sparks of negative influence, sparks that threaten to burn down a marriage, is one thing. Extinguishing the blaze is something entirely different.

It is critical that we:
- Pursue godly advice.
- Grow healthy friendships.
- Find experienced mentors.
- Learn from the successes and failures of others.

"The one who walks with the wise will become wise, but a companion of fools will suffer harm" (Proverbs 13:20, HCSB). Who is qualified to speak into your marriage?

Seek and gain wise counsel. Sound advice is like having a detailed map and a guide on a long, challenging journey. It can make the difference between the success or the destruction of a marriage.

You *can* choose to lead your heart. When you do, you safeguard your covenant relationships with God and your spouse. Your life and marriage become positive influences to others.

Pray continuously for your spouse and yourself.

- First and foremost, ask God to make His voice the most prominent influence in your life.
- Ask God to gear your mind, will, and emotions not to stop pursuing a God-honoring marriage.
- Confess that your heart can be influenced by lesser voices.
- Ask for help in seeking truth from God and to not be deceived by counterfeits.
- Petition God to bring people into your life— not just anyone but people who will guide you into a deeper love for God and for your spouse.

As you look for and receive these blessings, you will be living the dare to truly love.

A Love Dare

Based on Dare 2 in The Love Dare Journal

IN ADDITION TO SAYING NOTHING
NEGATIVE TO YOUR SPOUSE AGAIN
TODAY, DO AT LEAST ONE UNEXPECTED
GESTURE AS AN ACT OF KINDNESS.

LOVE NOTE: When things happen to cause you to be angry with your mate, race away from the temptation to think disapproving thoughts. You will be even less likely to let them come out in words.

You Can Honor and Cherish Your Spouse

REASON 3

Learn to rein in negative thoughts
about your spouse. Focus instead on
his or her positive attributes.
Doing so will help you honor your
marriage in your heart.

As you place your marriage under
the shade of God's unconditional love
for both of you, His love will become
your kind of love, an honoring
and cherishing love.

Don't let the culture around you determine the worth of your marriage. To compare it with something that can be discarded or replaced is to dishonor God's purpose for it. That would be like amputating a limb.

Instead, your marriage should be a picture of love between two imperfect people who choose to love each other regardless.

Whenever a husband looks into the eyes of his wife, he should remember that a man who loves his wife loves himself. And a wife should remember that when she loves her husband, she is also giving love and honor to herself.

Marriage partners should treat each other well. Speak highly of your spouse. Nourish and cherish the love of your life and watch your life grow because of it.

Thomas Jefferson said, "Nobody can acquire honor by doing what is wrong." Honor can be defined as holding someone in high esteem and viewing someone or something as rare or special. Too often we do the opposite of our commitment to honor and cherish by shaming, despising, and disrespecting our spouse.

God's Word instructs husbands to show their wives honor *"as co-heirs of the grace of life, so that your prayers will not be hindered"* (1 Peter 3:7, HCSB). Because

God loves us unconditionally, it matters to God when we place conditions on the love, honor, and respect we show each other.

Your spouse is as much a part of you as your hands, your eyes, or your heart. Honor, or the lack of it, becomes apparent in our conversations with one another—and with God. Our words, reactions, facial expressions, and tone of voice all shout a clear message to our spouses. That message is either, "You are priceless to me!" or "You are worthless to me!"

Jesus is the ultimate example of viewing people as priceless—valuable enough to die for. He related to each person He encountered through a lens of honor and respect. When you love and honor your spouse, you are honoring and respecting Christ. The opposite is also the case.

> *"Since you put away lying, speak the truth, each*
> *one to his neighbor, because we are members of*
> *one another. Be angry and do not sin. Don't let*
> *the sun go down on your anger, and don't give*
> *the Devil an opportunity. ...*
> *"No rotten talk should come from your mouth,*
> *but only what is good for the building up of*
> *someone in need, in order to give grace to*
> *those who hear."*

EPHESIANS 4:25-27,29, HCSB

You *can* choose to speak, act, and live in a manner that honors your spouse.

Words and actions are investments. Choose them carefully to increase their potential for helping your marriage succeed and honor God.

Closeness usually increases opportunities for conflict. But love can step in and remind you that your marriage is too valuable to allow it to self-destruct. Your love for your spouse is more important than whatever you're fighting about.

Love reminds you that conflict can be turned around for good. Married couples who learn to work through conflict tend to be more trusting and intimate, enjoying a much deeper connection going forward.

But how? The wisest way is to learn to fight clean. Establish healthy rules of engagement. If you don't have guidelines for how you'll approach hot topics, you won't stay in bounds when the action heats up.

SOME RULES OF ENGAGEMENT FOR CLEAN FIGHTING

Never mention divorce.

Never bring up unrelated items from the past.

Never fight in public or in front of your children.

Never forgo calling a "TIME OUT" if the conflict is becoming damaging.

Never touch one another in harmful ways.

Never go to bed angry with one another.

Never give up on working things out.

Pray that your Heavenly Father shows you how greater expressions of love and intimacy with your spouse will increase your love and intimacy with Him. Dare to take both relationships to a whole new level.

A Love Dare

Based on Dare 13 in The Love Dare Journal

TALK WITH YOUR SPOUSE ABOUT
ESTABLISHING HEALTHY RULES OF
ENGAGEMENT. IF YOUR MATE IS
NOT READY FOR THIS, THEN WRITE OUT
YOUR OWN PERSONAL RULES TO "FIGHT"
BY. RESOLVE TO ABIDE BY
THOSE RULES WHEN THE NEXT
DISAGREEMENT OCCURS.

LOVE NOTE: Think about your husband or wife's vulner-abilities. If you protect them when you argue, your spouse will likely trust you more. If you don't pursue a win at all costs mind-set, you may both take more time to listen to what is upsetting both of you.

You Can Live with Understanding

REASON 4

We enjoy discovering as much as we can about the things we really care about. You can choose to earn a life-long doctoral degree in the study of your spouse—a wonderfully complex creation of God.

Phileo and *eros*—Greek words referring to brotherly or friendship love and sexual love, respectively—describe the kinds of love that fluctuate with feelings or circumstances. *Agape* love, on the other hand, is selfless and unconditional. You are being challenged to "agape love" your spouse.

The Bible tells us in 1 John 4:10, "*Love consists in this: not that we loved God, but that He loved us and sent His Son to be the propitiation for our sins*" (HCSB).

Jesus gave His life so that everyone who believes in Him would be saved from God's wrath—which we deserve. God doesn't love us because we are lovable but because He is so loving. Unconditional love is God's kind of love.

Marriage can also be the basis for *agape*, or unconditional, love for our spouses. A lifetime commitment, coupled by a desire to understand the other person, helps bring clarity and depth to our lives.

The first chapter of the Gospel of Mark presents an incredible picture of Jesus, as He encountered a leper. In the first century a leper was considered an outcast, a reject who not only suffered a horrible, deadly disease but also debilitating loneliness. Yet when this man came to Jesus, the Lord showed compassion to him.

The Bible tells us Jesus felt compassion for the leper (Mark 1:40-45); however, the word *compassion* doesn't mean He merely felt sorry for the man. It doesn't mean pity. Even the word *empathy* falls short. The word *compassion* means to actually get in the middle of the mess. Jesus was moved to take on the burden of the leper.

Jesus doesn't just want to connect physically or emotionally with us. He wants to and will be in the middle of the wreck with us.

It is so hard for us to ask for help, even from our mates. We may think we deserve our trouble. But godly compassion says, "I'm not condemning you. I want you to trust my love for you, regardless."

Listening is one of the best ways to live with understanding, including to find out what's wrong in certain situations. Your spouse wants to know whether you are really listening.

Sometimes listening to your mate means *not*:

- giving advice
- trying to fix it
- defending your view
- even apologizing until your spouse knows you have fully heard the whole story
- assuming you know what your spouse feels about the matter

God knows secrets about us that we hide from ourselves! Yet He loves us at a depth we cannot begin to fathom.

How much more should we as imperfect people reach out to our spouses with grace and with understanding, assuring them that their secrets are safe with us?

A PRAYER FOR UNDERSTANDING

Lord Jesus, my Designer and King,
I pray for divine insight and inspiration in my life.
Give me the discernment I need to bless my family
and my spouse.

Teach us both to live by faith, having the ability
to navigate through difficult issues and hard times.

Give us communication that isn't just surface talk.
Help us to spend our words wisely and listen
with a heart of compassion.

You brought us together. You claimed us.
And we claim each other for Your glory. Amen.

A Love Dare

Based on Dare 18 in The Love Dare Journal

PREPARE A SPECIAL DINNER AT HOME,
JUST FOR THE TWO OF YOU. THE DINNER
CAN BE AS NICE AS YOU PREFER. FOCUS
THIS TIME ON GETTING TO KNOW
YOUR SPOUSE BETTER, PERHAPS IN
AREAS YOU'VE RARELY TALKED ABOUT.
DETERMINE TO MAKE IT AN ENJOYABLE
EVENING FOR YOU AND YOUR MATE.

LOVE NOTE: *During your dinner, consider asking these three questions to spark conversation.*

"What are three things that I do that you really like?"
"Who do you feel the most 'safe' being with and why?"
"What do you enjoy the most and the least about your life right now?"

(Taken from Appendix II, "20 Question for Your Spouse," *The Love Dare*, 206)

You Can Give Unconditional Love

REASON 5

You cannot give what you do not have.
You must have the love of Christ
before you can truly give
unconditional love to anyone else.
Christ's love is not based on merit,
circumstance, or consequence.
Seek a relationship with your
spouse that relentlessly, stubbornly,
sacrificially loves—
no matter what.

Sometimes life beats us up with a tragic loss, a major disappointment, or the death of someone close. In the middle of trouble, some couples pull together and others pull apart.

Every marriage experiences moments when love seems to fade. That's because we need someone who can give us unconditional love under every kind of pressure. God is the source of that kind of love—unconditional and overflowing.

He can give you a love for your spouse that you could never produce on your own. God wants to love your spouse through you.

God loves you and He is for you. He is not the enemy. And if you have never reached out to Him, please know that He has been reaching out to you your entire life.

"God proves His own love for us in that while we were still sinners Christ died for us!"

ROMANS 5:8, HCSB

Jesus tossed the old, self-preserving, me-first mind-set, calling us instead to be the most passionate curiously peculiar "lovers" the world has ever known. His is the kind of love that makes a practice and a life-style of unconditional love.

Such love goes deeper than appeasing, compro-mising, and tolerating. It runs beyond treaties, borders, and time limits. This kind of love is powerful and cou-rageous. The love of Jesus puts skin and bones on this life called Christianity.

> "I give you a new commandment: love one
> another. Just as I have loved you, you must also
> love one another."
>
> JOHN 13:34, HCSB

Practice this radical mission of unconditional love constantly, just as God loves you. Love whether or not the car works, your job is great, the garbage has been taken out, and your kids are sweet and admirable. Don't just camp in the wilderness of love; build your home there.

When you married, did you vow to love your spouse when you felt like it or in sickness and in health, for richer and for poorer, for better or for worse? A godly marriage is a metaphor of unconditional love.

This type of love is impossible apart from a close relationship with Jesus Christ. When we walk with Christ on a daily basis, His Holy Spirit pours out unconditional love in our hearts. Then we can love our spouse and others with that love. Jesus showed us what it takes to love this way.

> "As the Father has loved Me, I have also
> loved you; abide in My love.
> "If you keep My commandments, you will
> abide in My love; just as I have kept My
> Father's commandments and abide in His love."
>
> JOHN 15:9-10, NASB

Jesus is calling on you to accept that He loves you and to love Him back. When He becomes your source, then you will have the love it takes to value your marriage and to serve your spouse as a gift from the God you serve.

A Prayer for Selfless Love

Lord Jesus, Son of God,
How rich is Your mercy toward me!
How amazing Your grace! In times when
I turn my back on You, You relentlessly reach out
to me. So much love, Lord Jesus.
It is hard to take it all in.

Thank You, Jesus, Son of God.
Give me the courage to follow You.
From this day forward, love my mate through me.
Amen.

A Love Dare

Based on Dare 22 in The Love Dare Journal

LOVE IS A CHOICE, NOT A FEELING.
LOVE IS AN INITIATED ACTION, NOT A
KNEE-JERK REACTION. CHOOSE TODAY
TO BE COMMITTED TO LOVE EVEN IF
YOUR SPOUSE HAS LOST INTEREST IN
RECEIVING IT. TRY SAYING IN WORDS
SIMILAR TO THESE, "I LOVE YOU. PERIOD.
I CHOOSE TO LOVE YOU EVEN IF YOU
DON'T LOVE ME IN RETURN."

LOVE NOTE: *This kind of love is impossible without the love of Christ beating in your heart. His presence within you will enable you to love, even when love in your marriage seems very one-sided.*

You Can Walk
in Forgiveness

REASON 6

Complete forgiveness means
holding nothing between you and
your spouse and deciding,
"I will make a daily commitment to
practice forgiveness as a lifestyle."

Accidents happen. Sometimes we have to apologize for unintentional actions or outcomes. It's easy to get defensive when life is falling apart, to say, "I'm sorry, even though it wasn't my fault!"

Great marriages don't happen because couples stop sinning and failing each other. That's impossible. Great marriages happen because couples learn to never stop apologizing to and forgiving one another.

When couples don't forgive and mercy runs out, bad things begin to happen: harsh words, affairs, addictions, or even feeling like you have irreconcilable differences. One universal factor is required to turn any marriage around: COMPLETE FORGIVENESS.

> "Be kind and compassionate to one another,
> forgiving one another, just as God also forgave
> you in Christ."
>
> EPHESIANS 4:32, HCSB

Practice saying to yourself, *I will forgive others the same way that I want God to forgive me!* Then do it.

God doesn't skimp when it comes to forgiveness! The word *forgive* can also be understood as "pardon." Psalm 103:12 tells us, *"As far as the east is from the west, so far has He removed our transgressions from us"* (HCSB).

God plunges our sins into the depths of the sea.

> *"He will again have compassion on us; He will vanquish our iniquities. You will cast all our sins into the depths of the sea."*
>
> MICAH 7:19, HCSB

Forgiveness begins when you choose to treat another person the same way you want God to treat you. It's when you extend the same undeserved mercy that God extends to you.

Forgiveness happens when you let God be the Judge of another and you release all your anger and vengeance over to Him.

Refusing to forgive leads to anger, which leads to erosion of intimacy. Start leading your heart to forgive by taking one or all of the following actions:

- Ask God to show you why you do what you do.
- Confess so healing can begin.
- Extend undeserved mercy and forgiveness to anyone who has hurt you.
- Receive forgiveness by accepting God's forgiveness.
- Forgive yourself.
- Celebrate forgiveness with thankfulness and worship.
- Commit to never stop forgiving each other.
- Realize that forgiveness doesn't excuse the other person's deed.

With Christ in your life, you are free, forgiven, and ready to forgive. That's how you love your spouse unconditionally.

Does this all seem impossible to you? Ephesians 3:20 gives you the answer. "[He] *is able to do above and beyond all that we ask or think—according to the power that works in you*" (HCSB).

A Prayer for Forgiveness

Father, the greatest miracle in my life
is the wideness of Your forgiveness.
I am amazed by Your love for me.

I admit that there are times when I have wounded
and times when I have been wounded. I pray that
the grace, love, and forgiveness that flowed down
on me will also flow freely in my marriage.

Teach me how to forgive as I have been forgiven.
I pray that You will help me be the first
to initiate reconciliation in my home. Amen.

A Love Dare
Based on Dares 25 & 26 in The Love Dare Journal

PRAY THROUGH YOUR AREAS OF
WRONGDOING. ASK FOR GOD'S FOR-
GIVENESS; THEN HUMBLE YOURSELF
ENOUGH TO ASK YOUR SPOUSE FOR
FORGIVENESS AS WELL. WHATEVER
YOU HAVEN'T FORGIVEN IN YOUR MATE,
FORGIVE IT NOW. LET IT GO. JUST AS WE
ASK JESUS TO "FORGIVE US OUR DEBTS,"
EACH DAY WE MUST ASK HIM TO HELP
US "FORGIVE OUR DEBTORS."

LOVE NOTE: *If not forgiving is keeping you and your spouse in an emotional prison, start your escape with one sentence, "I choose to forgive."*

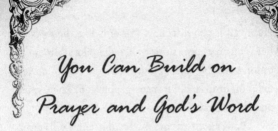

You Can Build on Prayer and God's Word

Marriage is God's beautiful,
priceless gift. By remaining teachable,
you learn to do the one thing that is
most important in marriage—to love
(1 Corinthians 13:3).
Placing all aspects of your marriage
under the authority of God's Word
and prayer is the greatest decision for
ultimate success in your marriage.

Prayer gives you direction. Prayer is like the rows of lights on an airport runway, like the pilot's communication with the control tower, like the plane's power to lift off or to land. Yet many people don't know what prayer is or how to begin.

Prayer is direct communication with God. Prayer works because it is a spiritual phenomenon created by God. And prayer yields amazing results.

Do you feel like giving up on your marriage? Jesus said to pray instead of quitting. Are you stressed out and worried? Prayer can bring peace to your storms. Do you need a major breakthrough? Prayer can make the difference.

Prayer does not have to be complicated or based on big religious words! It can be just you, simply sharing honestly with God about where you are and what you are feeling and needing. There's no reason to impress anyone during prayer. Just be humble and honest before God.

The (Not-So) Secret of Effective Praying

If you want to pray for your spouse and see your prayers answered, ask yourself:

- Is there anything I need to clear up with God?
- Is there anything the matter between others and me?
- Is my heart being honest with God, without selfish or hidden motives?

The Bible speaks to this type of prayer with a promise:

> "If our hearts do not condemn us, we have
> confidence before God, and can receive whatever
> we ask from Him because we keep His commands
> and do what is pleasing in His sight."
>
> 1 John 3:21-22, HCSB

Ask your spouse to pray with you. If you feel shy, start by joining hands and silently blessing a meal together. Or offer simple sentence prayers together. Tell God what you are concerned about or thankful for.

Prayer is sincere communication with Almighty God, the One who knows us and still loves us as a Father deeply loving His own children!

Building on the right foundation means spending time in God's Word, the Bible. God's Word is how He reveals himself to us.

Husbands and wives bring their own cultural traditions and family habits into marriage. They have ideas about how their new home should operate. The most unifying practice is to filter everything through the Word of God for direction on how to live as a couple and as a family.

The Bible is *"inspired by God and is profitable for teaching, for rebuking, for correcting, for training in righteousness, so that the man of God may be complete, equipped for every good work"* (2 Timothy 3:16-17, HCSB).

The Bible gives us:
- Guidance (Psalm 119:105)
- Wisdom (Psalm 119:97-100)
- Stability (Matthew 7:24-27)
- Freedom (John 8:32)
- Protection from temptation (Psalm 119:11)
- Success (Joshua 1:8)

Work demands, health issues, financial pressures, and in-law arguments can destroy your good marriage if you try to tackle these storms of life alone. You need a plan that incorporates prayer and God's Word into your marriage and home.

Think of your plan like a baseball game. To reach first base, begin praying for yourself each day. Second base is achieved when you start praying for your spouse and spending a few minutes exploring God's Word. Third base is reached when you invite your spouse to pray with you.

To score a run, also invite your household to pray with you and tell them what you are learning from God's Word. Now you are warmed up and ready to take it home and increase your score in the next inning of your life together.

Father God, I am so often tempted to act rather than pray! Forgive me the busy, distracted life that I often live outside the bounds of Your Word and Your voice. I choose today to seek You first. Amen.

A Love Dare

Based on Dare 37 in The Love Dare Journal

ASK YOUR SPOUSE IF YOU CAN BEGIN
PRAYING TOGETHER. TALK ABOUT THE
BEST TIME TO DO THIS, WHETHER IT'S
IN THE MORNING, YOUR LUNCH HOUR,
OR BEFORE BEDTIME. USE THIS TIME
TO COMMIT YOUR CONCERNS,
DISAGREEMENTS, AND NEEDS
BEFORE THE LORD.
DON'T FORGET TO THANK HIM FOR
HIS PROVISION AND BLESSING. EVEN
IF YOUR SPOUSE REFUSES TO DO THIS,
RESOLVE TO SPEND THIS DAILY TIME IN
PRAYER YOURSELF.

LOVE NOTE: Ask yourself what your mate would want if it were obtainable. Commit this to prayer. Enjoy the anticipation of your spouse's joy over an unexpected blessing.

You Can Establish a Covenant Marriage

REASON 8

Marriage is holy matrimony,
a covenant relationship in which God
is glorified. When your wedding vows
are expressed to God as well as to one
another, your marriage honors God
and is a testimony to others.

In marriage we learn a lot about each other through the daily activities of life. As you live out the principles of *The Love Dare*, life is the place to put these principles into action. Continue to lead your heart to forgive and honor and unconditionally love your spouse.

You will be able to tell if you are growing when you begin to:

- Make a positive impact on your marriage.
- Observe and affirm Christlikeness in your spouse.
- Value and rely on the input of your spouse as you face critical decisions together.

Marriage is viewed by some as just a piece of paper—a contract. They see it as merely a legal contract.

By definition, a contract sets legal accountability and limits liability; it makes certain that first and foremost our own issues are addressed; it ensures that someone adheres to certain minimum requirements. The contract must be in writing because it is built around distrust and can be broken by mutual consent.

On the other hand, while marriage is more than a business agreement, even writing our own vows shows we have begun to define marriage in our own terms. But marriage was created by God. He joins a man and woman together as one. For God to "witness" our vows means that the vows we make to our spouse we are also making to God.

In a wedding, a covenant or a promise is being made between the bride, the groom, and God. It is a promise that is not to be broken—ever.

God always takes marriage promises seriously:

> "And this is another thing you do: you cover the
> Lord's altar with tears, with weeping and
> groaning, because He no longer respects your
> offerings or receives [them] gladly from your
> hands. Yet you ask, 'For what reason?'
> "Because the Lord has been a witness between
> you and the wife of your youth. You have acted
> treacherously against her, though she was your
> marriage partner and your wife by covenant."
>
> Malachi 2:13-14, HCSB

Throughout history, God has initiated loving, trusting, permanent relationships with His people. He makes verbal promises called *covenants* for our good—promises He never has broken and never will break. Our God is a covenant-making God and has left a record of His promises in the Bible.

COVENANTS IN THE BIBLE

NOAH
God promised to never again destroy all humanity by flood.

ABRAHAM
An entire nation would come from his descendants.

MOSES
Israel would be God's special people.

DAVID
The Messiah would come from his lineage and that Ruler would sit on David's throne forever.

NEW COVENANT
The sacrifice of Jesus on the cross provides forgiveness and eternal life to all who believe.

Jesus said of husbands and wives:

"So they are no longer two but one flesh.
Therefore, what God has joined together,
man must not separate."

MATTHEW 19:6, HCSB

And, from the ancient Book of Genesis:

> "Then the LORD God made the rib He had
> taken from the man into a woman and
> brought her to the man. And the man said:
> This one, at last, is bone of my bone, and flesh
> of my flesh; this one will be called woman,
> for she was taken from man.
> "This is why a man leaves his father and
> mother and bonds with his wife, and they
> become one flesh."
>
> GENESIS 2:22-24, HCSB

And the beauty of practicality:

> "Two are better than one because they have a
> good reward for their efforts. For if either falls,
> his companion can lift him up; but pity the one
> who falls without another to lift him up."
>
> ECCLESIASTES 4:9-10, HCSB

Covenant marriage not only provides support for each spouse but also for children. God's plan for procreation is within the one-flesh, for-a-lifetime covenant of marriage. That is why marriage vows are premeditated, publicly spoken, and witnessed by others. These serious promises are legally binding, spiritually binding, and physically binding.

Ironically, the solemn vows and heavy expectations of covenant weddings are the basis for the trust and hopes that make marriage fun. Covenant marriage takes the joy men and women find in their mates to deeper, more enriching dimensions.

When a couple lives out their marriage in this way, it is truly holy matrimony. Scripture teaches that covenant marriage is a clear picture of the relationship between Christ and the church.

When your covenant vows are vertical, expressed to God as well as to your spouse, then your marriage becomes a testimony to the world of the glory of God.

HUSBAND: What would happen in your marriage if you were to completely devote yourself to loving, honoring, and serving your wife in all things?

WIFE: What would happen in your marriage if you made it your mission to do everything possible to respect and promote togetherness of heart with your husband?

Love is what happens when two people commit themselves to one another. First Corinthians 13:8 tells us, "*Love never ends.*" That's what Jesus' love is like.

His disciples were nothing if not unpredictable. Yet Jesus never stopped loving them because He and His love are "*the same yesterday, today, and forever*" (Hebrews 13:8, HCSB).

When you have done everything within your power to obey God, your spouse may still forsake you and walk away, just as Jesus' followers did to Him. But if your marriage fails, if your spouse walks away, let it not be because you gave up or stopped loving. Let God love through you.

Love never ends.

A PRAYER FOR
COVENANT MARRIAGE

Father,
We are a couple who wants to follow You
in authentic relationships and covenant.

We need You to sharpen our vision and restore
the brokenness we encounter deep
within our spirits.
We need the unity that only You can bring.

We need to follow You with unswerving loyalty
so we are asking for Your strength and the
transformation that is offered in Your world.

Without You, how can we promise anything?
We are desperately dependent on You.
Give us passion and strength
to fireproof our marriages.
In the name of Jesus, Amen.

A Love Dare

Based on Dare 39 in The Love Dare Journal

SPEND TIME IN PERSONAL PRAYER;
THEN WRITE A LETTER OF COMMIT-
MENT AND RESOLVE TO YOUR SPOUSE.
INCLUDE WHY YOU ARE COMMITTING
TO THIS MARRIAGE UNTIL DEATH, AND
THAT YOU HAVE PURPOSED TO LOVE
HIM OR HER NO MATTER WHAT. LEAVE
THE LETTER IN A PLACE WHERE YOUR
MATE WILL BE SURE TO FIND IT.

LOVE NOTE: *You can't know for sure how your spouse will respond to this letter. Stay focused on what it has meant to you to write it. No matter how your spouse responds or reacts, be happy that you have offered him or her these thoughts as a gift and a promise. Remember, you have had time to think through intentionally strengthening your marriage. Allow your spouse time to think it through also.*

Conclusion

Learning to truly love is one of the most important things you will ever do. We challenge you to take *The Love Dare* and *The Love Dare Bible Study* and experience the full 40-day adventure for yourself. Hopefully your spouse will join you and a few like-minded couples so that together you will become a community of people who know the value of love and investing in your marriage. See for yourself how other marriages are being transformed (*www.lovedare.bhpublishinggroup.com*).

When you walk with God, He will put dreams in your heart that He wants to fulfill in your life. He will also put skills and abilities in your heart that He wants to develop for His glory (see Exodus 35:30-35).

As you put God first, He will step in and fulfill the good desires of your heart. The Bible says, "*Delight yourself in the Lord; and He will give you the desires of your heart*" (Psalm 37:4, NASB). Know that the only time you can feel good about following your heart is when your heart is intent on serving and pleasing God.

DARE TO TAKE GOD
AT HIS WORD

The ultimate decision you can make is to
dare to take God at His Word. Dare to trust
Jesus Christ for your personal salvation.

Dare to pray:

"Lord Jesus, I'm a sinner.
But You have shown Your love for me
by dying to forgive my sins, and
You have proven Your power to save
me from death by Your resurrection.

"Lord, forgive my sin and
change my heart, and
save me by Your grace."

For more information about becoming a Christian
or to share your decision, please contact LifeWay
Christian Resources. We would love to
assist and celebrate with you!

www.lifeway.com

Is your church fireproofed?

The success of the movie *FIREPROOF* sparked a lot of conversation. But *The Love Dare Bible Study* adds the power of Scripture and provocative questions to get a group really talking. And we've seen much more than one happy ending. Is your church ready to take the love dare? Order online, call 800.458.2772, or visit the LifeWay Christian Store serving you.

ireproof

LifeWay | Adults

About the Authors

STEPHEN KENDRICK serves as senior associate pastor of preaching and prayer at Sherwood Baptist Church, Albany, Georgia. He and his brother, Alex, co-wrote *The Love Dare* (B&H Publishing Group), a 40-day challenge for spouses to understand and practice unconditional love, and *The Love Dare Bible Study*. Stephen co-wrote and produced *Fireproof* (2008).

ALEX KENDRICK is the associate pastor of movie outreach at Sherwood Baptist Church and oversees the film ministry. He teaches a weekly televised Bible study program called *Home Connection*. *Fireproof* is the third movie directed by Alex and co-written with his brother, Stephen.

MICHAEL CATT is the senior pastor of Sherwood Baptist Church and Executive Producer for Sherwood Pictures' films *Flywheel*, *Facing the Giants*, and *Fireproof*. Sherwood Pictures is the moviemaking ministry of Sherwood Baptist Church.